T0065517

LIVE & LEARN /
LEARN & LIVE

Lessons from men & Godly mentors

ART PHINNEY

WESTBOW
P R E S S®
A DIVISION OF THOMAS NELSON
& ZONDERVAN

This book is a work of non-fiction. Unless otherwise noted, the author and the publisher make no explicit guarantees as to the accuracy of the information contained in this book and in some cases, names of people and places have been altered to protect their privacy.

WestBow Press books may be ordered through booksellers or by contacting:

WestBow Press
A Division of Thomas Nelson & Zondervan
1663 Liberty Drive
Bloomington, IN 47403
www.westbowpress.com
844-714-3454

Scripture taken from the New King James Version®. Copyright © 1982 by Thomas Nelson. Used by permission. All rights reserved.

ISBN: 978-1-6642-6649-0 (sc)
ISBN: 978-1-6642-6650-6 (hc)
ISBN: 978-1-6642-6648-3 (e)

Library of Congress Control Number: 2022908806

Print information available on the last page.

WestBow Press rev. date: 05/14/2022

DEDICATION

To my precious and amazing wife Sherry, who's love, and devotion has carried on and continues to do so at this moment.

To the late Don Levi and Chuck Smith. To George Stathos and finally Carl Westerlund – School of Ministry (SoM). Four pastors in my life who encouraged me to move forward in God's calling.

To the countless men, some are named in this book, who have been an instrument in the hand of God to shape this wayward boy into a God seeking man.

PREFACE

FROM CRADLE TO GRAVE

He had been silent on the way to the hospital. Although he'd been propped up and in his car seat he wasn't saying much. Earlier on the phone, the advice nurse had clearly said: "…keep talking to him and don't let him fall asleep…" As I made the twenty-minute drive into town all I could do was pray, sing and talk as much as I could believing we would make it!

David was only three at the time. Somehow, he had found his way to a bottle of children's Co-Tylenol. This was back in the day before safety lids, and I had not properly secured the cupboard. As I recall it there were twenty-three pills missing. Panic struck and I got on the phone to ask a nurse what I should do. "Bring him in" she replied, that was the directive. Once David and I arrived at the hospital I was quickly informed that they would need to "pump" his stomach and remove as much of the medicine as they could. I gave my consent and into a clean triage room we went. They laid my three-year-old down on the table while I held his hand and spoke words of comfort as often as I could.

First, the clear small tube was lubricated with gel and then inserted into his left nostril and forced down into the small intestine. Next, a medium syringe was attached to the tube and they began the "extraction" protocol. Basically, it meant that each time they pulled up on the syringe David would feel as though he was vomiting. Then little pink particles of Children's Co-Tylenol would appear in the syringe for discarding. Then we'd do it all over again and again. Ouch!

At one point David looked up at me and yelled: "Dad, mak'em stop!" It was in that moment that I learned a lesson. I could've lied and told him that I will. But I knew that wasn't true and I didn't ever want to lie to him. I could've told him I can't and face the obvious fact that his "dad" is not superman with all power! (We all know that's not true either but many of us young fathers like to give our young boys that impression!)

So, I decided on a truthful compromise. I said this: "… I will as soon as I can." Which meant that as soon as they'd saved his life, I can ask them to stop! (smile) Yes,

David made it through that night resting peacefully. I continued to thank the medical staff for their concern and professional help. And I understood that night that there will always be things to learn.

From the cradle until we enter the grave we've been set upon a path of learning. We all have. We learn to cry when troubled and hurt, eat when hungry, smile when glad and on it goes. The question becomes are you living better and or smarter because of the things you've learned?

Especially for the child of God there are necessary things that each of us must learn once we come to faith in Christ! As a babe does in the physical world so the babe in Christ does in the Spiritual world. We learn to walk, sit and finally to run. But who is our teacher? The Bible informs us the Holy Spirit will teach us all things that Jesus has said. But often in life the lessons that God will teach us come to us through the people in our lives.

This book is simply a record of many of the men that God has used to instruct me in various ways. Each one of them is infinitely more precious than the lesson I learned from them, but I remain grateful for the lesson as well. My hope for the reader is that they will find a bit of themselves in these accounts and perhaps even learn for themselves some valuable and tangible lessons that help them along their way.

That's what this book is all about.

"…For whatever things were written before were written for our learning, that we through the patience and comfort of the Scriptures might have hope." (Ro 15:4)

CONTENTS

GRANDPA JENSON – A FORK AT THE TABLE

1957-1960

WHAT WAS YOUR GRANDFATHER LIKE? Did you know either of them? Meaning either the one on your mother and/or father's side? Many of us remember at least one. I only knew the one on my mother's side. Mine was a jewel. But a jewel has many sides through which the light can pass. Even through a fork at the table. Let me explain.

My grandfather, we'll call him Grandpa Jenson or GJ for short was a faithful husband, a father in his home and the main provider for his household. Arthur Leroy Jenson, from whom I received my first name, served as a postal service worker in Oakland, CA, after moving down from Pasco, Washington in the late 1940's to buy a home and find work in a post WWII era. It was there that he raised his two daughters. My aunt, Thelma, and his eldest, our mom, Marjorie. Grandpa never had a son. Perhaps that's why he was so, shall we say, intentional in his attempts to discipline my brother and I when we were very young.

My childhood years in Oakland with GJ are a blur. As I recall we moved nine times within the first 6 years of my elementary schooling. If you think that is a lot you would be right. His daughter, our mom, had become a single mom early. Raising two boys, she did her very best at keeping us in line. But we needed a man's presence in our lives and GJ was up to bat much of the time. At one point in these many moves we lived in a place called the Projects. The "Projects" were a low-income group of apartments sitting off East 14th Street at Heaven's Court Boulevard. It was walking distance to grandpa's house in those days when it was still relatively safe to walk that area. I recall many fond memories at our grandparents' home. Birthday's, holidays, and Christmas Eve were often celebrated there. That meant many meals at the table. More about that later. As I mentioned, our mom was a single mom from the time she had a three-year-old and a newborn and was either working or looking for work. That situation required the help of our grandparents. In the early 1950's this was not so much the norm.

As I write this memoir, I too am a father and grandfather! I too have experienced the joy and challenge of a daughter's need to "move back in with mom and dad!" The reasons for any one of my daughter's temporarily returning home were most simply due to difficult life circumstances. The point here is that when they returned, they came back with children! Those children were our precious grandchildren at very young ages.

Having experienced it I can instantly relate to Grandpa Jenson. There you are, your adult daughter with her own living habits, now a single mom with children and her own ways of dealing with them, squeezed into your living quarters to share all things! It takes the grace of God for it to go well and for us it went very well. But it was always clear that this mom, our daughter, could benefit from help with her children. What mom doesn't, single or not? So, as a father and a grandfather you step in. When you see a child, your grandchild may I remind us, needing correction you correct. When you see that child needing teaching or direction, you teach and direct. And when you see that child needing discipline for wrong choices made, it's time to apply it!

After all, isn't that what our Heavenly Father does? He will use His word to do these same things in our lives if we'll let Him. Paul tells his son in the faith, Timothy that: "All Scripture is given by inspiration of God, and is profitable for doctrine, for reproof, for correction, for instruction in righteousness …". (2 Tim.3:16). Do you see it? Teaching, instruction and correction and discipline!

So back to Grandpa Jenson. There we were at the dinner table one night in our grandparents' home. A lovely table setting, and meal served. Grandma always seemed to set the table nice for dinner. Grandpa was one for making sure children, especially two rowdy boys, understood proper table manners. Hands where they should be, please and thank you and eat what is on your plate without complaining. It may sound old school, I know, but it's still so needed today. We, my brother, and I had been corrected and instructed in these things many times before this night. But on this night, something special took place!

The adults were eating, and this child started to play with his food without an eating utensil in his hand. All the sudden GJ's hand reached across the table and with one loving, gentle but firm, smack with his fork on my hand taught me what I should and should not be doing while at his table. I was very young and don't remember the exact circumstances, but I'll tell you this. I've never forgotten my table manners since. I've also grown to appreciate and respect what Grandpa Jenson was trying to do that night more so now than ever.

Today, as I see so many young way-ward boys heading in poor directions and when I observe young boys in need of correction and discipline, so many fathers absent in the homes, I thank God for my grandfather. As far as I know he was not a professing Christian. I don't remember him ever going to church. I never saw a Bible in his hands, but I know this. God used him to teach me. It just took a while for me to get it! Thanks, gramps, for the fork at the table.

Who is it that God may be using to teach you today? Who is it in your life path that perhaps God wants you to step in and offer some direction or instructions too? Take some time to think about it and ask God what HE might have you to do.

KEN POORE / HUME LAKE – " ...WHAT DID YA DO THAT FOR?"

1967-1968

I AM ALWAYS SURPRISED THAT SMALL parts of my life's story are often mirrored in so many other people's lives. Consider the musical legend: Michael W. Smith! While reading his book, "The Way of The Father" I was struck by the events that surrounded his teenage years. No spoilers here but I do recommend the book to every reader. My teenage years have a similar curve that I'd like to share. It starts at Hume Lake Christian Camp, north of Fresno California and with a man named Ken Poore.

On the invitation of a cousin, I traveled with a church youth group to a summer camp for a week. I did not grow up going to church and really had no understanding about the gospel or what a Christian Summer Camp was all about. Whatever it was that made me desire to go came from outside of myself. Honestly, in hindsight, it was the Spirit of God. I was a wayward young man looking for direction at age 15.

The weeklong experience was filled with rope swings, horse rides, trail hikes, swimming and tons of short bible studies! In the mornings before breakfast hundreds of teens all met in a hall for something called a "morning devotion!" Most mornings I had no idea what was going on or what was being said. When devotions were over it was chow time and breakfast always sounded good! After breakfast it was time for those fun events to begin. Each day ended with a Fireside gathering, outdoor amphitheater style and a presentation of what they called: "the good news of the gospel." I don't recall an invitation to respond given until the last night of the week. This is where Ken Poore comes in.

Ken Poore was an official fixture at Hume Lake Christian Camp for many years during the 1960's and 70's. His friendly mannerism and genuine love for young adults was contagious. He was a large build guy that was unmistakable in a crowd. This becomes very important later on. All week long he would gently appeal to the young at heart about the life that was ahead of us. Reminding us that there was a God who created us, loves us and has a plan for our lives. Some of us were listening and some of us were not. I was not until that Friday night anyway!

There we were in the mountain air, fireside glowing, and saying goodbye to a week of great experiences and new friends. Ken Poore began the evening by leading us in a song or two. The word of God had been constantly placed before us each morning and evening encouraging us to believe in God and the Son of God, Jesus Christ! There is a verse in Romans 10:17 that says;

"So then faith comes by hearing, and hearing by the word of God." and, boy oh boy, had we been hearing the word. As Mr. Poore began his closing message it was as if the voice of Jesus was calling out through this man who was willing to be God's mouthpiece. I don't remember a lot of details about that moment, but I do know that Ken talked about the reality of heaven and hell. He taught from the book of Revelation that affirms the promise of an eternal destiny awaiting every human being and the choosing of that destiny being our choice to make. He quoted something Jesus had said: *"Behold, I stand at the door and knock. If anyone hears My voice and opens the door, I will come in to him and dine with him, and he with Me."* (Rev. 3:20)

I'm telling you, I could hear Him knocking at the door of my heart that night! The question was, would

I open and let Him in? Where would I choose to spend eternity when I die? Apart from God in hell or at His side in Heaven?

The choice is always ours. God will never "force Himself" upon anyone. When the invitation came to receive the forgiveness of Christ and the promise of Heaven, I knew I needed to answer. Before I knew it, I had raised my hand, then I was standing with many others and finally we all were asked to come down next to the fireside. Each one of us who had responded to Ken's invitation that night stood there in front of hundreds of other teens, we were unsure of what all we'd just said yes too. Then, we closed our eyes and Ken led us in a prayer of salvation. When I opened my eyes, I could tell something miraculous had just happened. I was saved! Thank you, Jesus! I did not know what it all meant but I knew it was real! The promise comes also from the book of Romans. *"…that if you confess with your mouth the Lord Jesus and believe in your heart that God has raised Him from the dead, you will be saved. For with the heart one believes unto righteousness, and with the mouth confession is made unto salvation."* (Romans 10:9-10 NKJV)

When I returned to my home and friends, I had trouble explaining what had happened to me that night. I would say things like: "I met Jesus" and "I'm born again" all of which were very true but really confused my buddies because they were not a part of my experience. They were "happy for me" but they also wanted me to continue doing some of the "not so good" things I had done with them before I left. That is always the dilemma with a new believer and old friends.

Without any follow up from the youth group leaders, and no attending the sponsoring church, the experience began to fade. If you add to those circumstances taking no time in a bible to be discipled and no encouragement at home to read a bible or go to church to grow in my newfound faith, my enlightened mind fell back to what I'd known before. Searching, searching and many more years of searching. This is where I tell every reader that considers themselves a Christian about the importance of reading your bible, going to a bible teaching church and finding a small group of other Christians to spend time with. It's so important!

I'm pretty sure that if I had died in a car wreck or something during those early years I would have ended up in heaven. (depending upon your theological position) But other than that there was no real relationship with Jesus going on and in the many years of trouble that followed. Perhaps I knew Him as a Savior, but I did not know Him as Lord! But before you let out a load sigh of disappointment … there is a sweet redeeming part to this story.

Fast forward some 15 years later and living in Lodi, CA. At age 27, I had bottomed out on my fruitless and endless searching and re-committed my life to Christ. Here is what happened.

One night, while camping in Yosemite and uniquely enough sitting by a campfire, I knew my life was empty and lacked real purpose! My painful years of searching had included deep alcoholism, drug addictions and constantly trying to find fulfillment. So, that night, through tears I asked God, if He was real, to come and take over. Obviously, left to my own choices, I was making a wreck of things. To my utter amazement, He did! My life truly began to change after that night and has continued to change still today. He can do the same for you. If you ask Him with a sincere heart, He'll meet you right where you are. No matter how far you've wondered, how far you drift or how many things you've done that might seem unforgivable. He'll welcome your repentance, forgive you all over again and then take up residence in your heart! But it gets better!

A few years after that second campfire evening, something else amazing happened! I heard that a man named Ken Poore was coming to visit a local church near where I lived. I couldn't believe it! Could this be true that the same man that had led me to Christ 15 years earlier was going to speak? I decided to go and marked my calendar. Once the evening came and as I was driving into the parking lot, I noticed a car in front of me. I also noticed that it was being driven by a large build, single man! Oh my, I thought: "Could it be?" How would that be for divine appointments? I parked right next to the same car. Then I looked at him to confirm my suspicions trying not to be too obvious.

Well, you guessed it. As Ken Poore stepped out of his vehicle, I matched him in stride walking up to the church slightly behind him. As we drew close to the front doors, I took a big gulp and said, " ...Excuse me but are you Ken Poore?" He stopped, turned and greeted me very kindly. Its what happened next that is the whole point of this story. Let me explain.

It took about two minutes to go from the parking lot to the church doors. In that short amount of time, I tried to fast-track him on my salvation experience with him at Hume Lake, the unstable searching years that followed and how I had just recently returned to that decision to follow Christ that I had made so long ago. I'm sure I was over apologetic to him for the bad choices I had made during those searching years. And yet, with the tenderness of a loving father figure he took my arm, turned me sideways, gave me a symbolic swift but very gentle kick in the rear and said; *"...well what did ya do that for?"* *"Welcome home son, lets go in and enjoy the Lord together."* With that we parted ways.

That night in Lodi and pastor Ken's words have stuck with me forever. God used Ken's joyful question to cause me to reevaluate the choices I made through the years after Hume Lake. I really had no answer for " …what did ya do that for" except for the obvious conclusion that I was, for a long time, unwilling to make Christ the Lord of my life. I had known Him as a Savior but, on that night, I was walking with Him as my Lord.

The timeline goes a bit like this. Hume Lake took place in the summer of 1967, It was the summer between 8th and 9th grade. I re-dedicated my life to Jesus Christ in 1980. Ken and I talked in 1983. Today, in 2021, I've been enjoying walking with the Lord for some 41 years.

Here is what I will ask you. Are you still resisting the love and direction of a Heavenly Father? What for? Jesus said: "Behold, I stand at the door and knock. If anyone hears My voice and opens the door, I will come in to him and dine with him, and he with Me. (Rev. 3:20). Is He knocking on the door of your heart today to let Him in and your hesitating? I'll ask you the same question that Ken asked me: ***What would ya do that for?*** Perhaps you are waiting for another moment in time. Don't wait any longer, don't miss another moment with Him. Invite this One who you may know as a Savior to now be your Lord.

BEN TIAPON – GOD'S PROVIDENCE / A REAL JOB MIRACLE

1981

SHORTLY AFTER RE-COMMITTING MY LIFE to Christ in 1980, the fact that I was 27 and had no skill or career path became amazing important. During my searching years I had dropped out of high school and had no degree. I was always "floating" from one job to another. For a while I had painted the exterior of homes, but my various bad choices allowed that to fall apart. I worked in an Orchard Supply Hardware for a very short time, only to lose that job because of tardiness. Finally, I had landed a starting position at a hamburger joint cleaning the floors at night! At this point I knew I needed to excel and get promoted to higher positions or find a better paying job.

Fortunately, God was very gracious to me. I quickly found favor in the owner's eyes and worked my way into a management position within the first three years. The name of the hamburger stand was Hambrick's 1/4lb Giant Burgers in Oakland. They had four or five locations in the bay area. I was grateful for the job and willing to "bloom where I was planted" but I also knew this was a low paying career path.

As a young Christian I was finding great truths in the bible. Somewhere in the bible I had read the Jesus hears us when we pray to Him. I think it was in Psalm 86:7 which says, " ...In the day of my trouble I will call upon You, For You will answer me." So, I began to trust Him to hear my prayer for a better paying job and life direction. Then it happened.

One day while cooking the lunch rush at Hambrick's, some burly looking guys came in and ordered burgers from the counter. As they watched me handle the grill something prompted them to ask me a question. This is where the providence of God comes in which simply means that He, God Almighty, is going ahead of you in life, creating situations and relationships that He will use to bless you.

Back to the question they asked me. The question went something like this: " ...*how would you like a real job?*" I blushed and then quietly asked: " ...*doing what?*" It's not very loyal to be managing for one employer while asking about a different job. (smile) Their answer was an invitation to become a meat cutter for Lucky Stores. Through a little more conversation, I found out that the starting pay was extremely higher than what I was currently making, and it promised advancement and pension! I asked them: " ...*what do I do to get on?*" They proceeded to scratch the phone number of the area Supervisor, Ben Tiapon, on a piece of paper. When I served them their burgers, they handed me the number with some advice: "*keep trying, he's busy but if he knows your serious you might eventually get an interview!*"

It took almost four months and many attempts to catch up with him, but he agreed to let me come into the San Lorenzo Lucky Store and fill out an application. After filling out the paperwork, the store manager says; "we'll put it on file" and Ben will get back to me some time! That's it? He'll get back to me in time. Boy, was I going to have to learn some patience here?

But sure enough, the call came from Ben, and I was asked to come in and interview with him there at San Lorenzo. Ben's questions caused me to think about why I wanted to work for Lucky's. God used this man to force me to think in a mature way about the present and the future! The interview lasted about twenty minutes and then he said: " ...we have your application and I'll let you know when there is an opening." It was another exercise in patience and faith. It took another month until Ben's next call came. "Art, we are ready to hire you and I want to to report to the store on Monday morning at 7:00 a.m. to finish the paperwork and start your job!"

I was completely beside myself. God had not only heard my prayer but answered it in a way that was over and above all I could have ever hoped or thought. It was a miracle! A Lucky Store's real job miracle. Now, you might think it strange for a young man to think getting a job is a miracle but remember where I had come from. So many previously bad choices leading to poor ends. So undeserving of such kindness. But that is who our Savior, Jesus Christ is. Full of kindness and grace.

One side note that reinforces that fact that it was actually a miracle. In 1983, I became the "oldest" apprentice butcher that Lucky Stores had every hired! My apprenticeship lasted two years and at age 30 I became a journeyman meat cutter. I served at Lucky Stores for over thirteen and a half years and God used those various meat cutting rooms as a place to mature me, test me, teach me and humble me with lesson's that are lasting my entire life.

Have you trusted Christ with your life? If so His "providence" is at work right now. He's involved in your decision making and going ahead of you to create situations and relationships designed to bless you. Have you asked Him to meet that very important need in your life? Ask, then be patient and watch Him answer in a way that is over and above all that you could have ever hoped or imagined!

Ephesians 3:20-21 says it so perfectly; "Now to Him who is able to do exceedingly abundantly above all that we ask or think, according to the power that works in us ... to Him be glory in the church by Christ Jesus to all generations, forever and ever. Amen."

DICK MILLS – A LIFE VERSE FROM THE SCRIPTURE

1981

IMAGINE THIS WITH ME. YOU'RE sitting somewhere with a friend and all the sudden God comes down, stands near you, points in your direction, and speaks a promise to you from a chapter and verse in His word! What would you do? How would you react? Don't answer that yet. Not until you hear the rest of the story so let's back up.

By now you have come to know a little bit about my childhood background. Fatherless, the younger of two boys, our mom was a single mom working to provide for her kids. Oakland, California was a decent place to grow up and it certainly had it's rough areas but in the late 1950's and early 1960's it actually had some real charm as well. One such charming area were the East Oakland hills and the 6th grade Elementary School I attended.

Early throughout my childhood I was introduced to music. Our mom loved to sing and would often sing along with some of her favorites playing on a radio. My introduction to playing a musical instrument came in the 6th grade. It was at Burckhalter Elementary School where I was invited to learn to play the Coronet. My music class was small enough for me to receive one on one instruction from the band teacher and our mom was willing to "rent" an instrument from the local music store. It was a very fun year. Not long after I had started learning to play, I heard about a "talent" show coming for each class and immediately had an idea. I could lip sync to Louise Armstrong's classic, "Hello Dollie" and represent my 6th grade class. Wouldn't that be fun? So, with a white handkerchief in one and my coronet in the other I gave it my best shot. I was 12 years old. In today's "Cancel Culture" and things like, "Black Live's Matter" I imagine those groups might have a few things to say about a white male imitating a black singer on a stage! But let's get back to the point. Playing an instrument and singing in front of people (although I was faking it at that time) became a part of what I would do the rest of my life. It became a door through which the best of things and the worst of things were allowed to enter into my world.

The next privilege came when I auditioned for the Oakland City Boys Choir. During the summer of 6th-7th grade I heard about this opportunity through school and my mom, once again, agreed to let me try. Once I was accepted into the Choir it meant weekly practices and a few recitals. I learned a lot about vocal work and a little bit about working with others. It was indeed fun to follow a Choral Director's instruction and learn to sing harmony! It also was a very fun summer.

Then came 7th grade in Jr High School. King Jr High to be exact. And it was such an eye opener for every one of us freshman. But, as providence would have it, the Jr High School Band had room for one more trumpet player. My 7th grade stretch in that school band was a prelude to changing instruments. By the 8th grade Mr. Ono, our tremendous band leader, asked me to consider switching to Tuba! Yep, you heard it right, Tuba. His reasons were simple. There were seven trumpet players and all of them were better than me. There was only "one" Tuba player, and he needed a second. Mr. Ono could tell I was a bit directionless in life and his encouragement found a willing soul.

So, off to the music store we went. We traded the coronet for a tuba and signed up for lessons. I can still remember carrying that big old Concert Tuba and its case down 82nd avenue after school every Tuesday for my tuba lesson. By the way, that year our band went on to win second place in the California Jr High Regional competitions. We even contracted with a recording company to come to the school and help us make an album. Our score was: Theme from Romeo And Juliet! We all felt like recording stars.(smile) But there I was playing an instrument in front of people again and this time I wasn't lip-syncing it!

The Jr. High School band days were short lived but playing music (and singing) in front of people was not. By the summer of 8th grade my friends and I had started a rock and roll band.

Remember Hume Lake and Ken Poore? (see above) One of the guys was over 18 but the rest of us were minors.

Believe it or not, after 5 or 10 rehearsals and with a few recommendations from some older garage band guys down the street, we were given our first gig! That "gig" was playing cover songs at the Alameda Naval Base Enlisted Men's Club on a Tuesday night. That's right, Jr High School age kids playing in a bar. I still don't understand who allowed that one to slip by, but we each made $50 bucks that night. We all thought we'd made it rich! I dropped the tuba and the school band to become the drummer of all things. But there I was playing and singing in front of people again. A pattern was beginning to appear! (smile).

The rock and roll years have their own sorted stories and lasted the better part of 12 years but suffice to say it was all a continuation of playing and singing in front of people. Repeatedly! This pattern that started when I was quite young would stick with me.

So, maybe by now, you're wondering what all of this has to do with Dick Mills and a life verse from scripture? Ok, fast forward to re-dedicating my life to Christ at age 27 in the mountains of Yosemite. After 12 years of playing and singing in front of people exclusively for secular or un-Godly purposes, my involvement in the music field was taking a major change in direction.

It was a Sunday evening service at a local church that was serving as my home church now that Jesus was my Lord as well as my Savior. That morning, the congregation had been told that a special evangelist with the gift of the word of wisdom and word of knowledge was coming tonight. His name was Dick Mills. If you are wondering what a "word of wisdom or knowledge" is I can best direct you to 1 Corinthians 12:8 in the bible. There it explains that those are gifts of the Holy Spirit. It is basically an insight into a person's life given by the Holy Spirit. God gives the insightful word of wisdom or knowledge to a person to speak to another. I have since learned (over 40 years of ministry) that Dick Mills was well respected in his gifting and not a heretic at all.

After a brief message about the Holy Spirit and His gifts to the body of Christ, pastor Dick Mills began to minister to us in a very special way. He would look right out at folks seated, he would point to them, ask them their name, and then speak a word of wisdom or word of knowledge over them. Then it happened! Sure, enough he pointed at me and he asked me my name and I told him, "Art."

Then he proceeded to give me this verse from the book of Isaiah. *"For you shall go out with joy, And be led out with peace; The mountains and the hills Shall break forth into singing before you, And all the trees of the field shall clap their hands."* (Isaiah 55:12).

Do you see it? This guy had never met me before. He had no idea of my background and history of singing or playing. And yet, under the inspiration of the Holy Spirit, he spoke this word that was so fitting to me at the present and my future.

I didn't understand the deep application of that word at that moment. In fact, it would take years before I fully understood it. What I believed God's word to be saying and what I received from that promise of God that night is simply this.

That my musical life, now as a Christian, would be filled with the worship of God while singing and playing an instrument. And it would be those lifelong combined acts of worshiping God that He would use to usher His peace and joy into my life daily. Because of it I would: *"…go out with joy and be led out with peace!"* I also came to understand that much of this would take place in front of others. Or as the verse declares *"…trees of the field."* And that others would sing along with me and clap their hands while doing so. *"…mountain and hills shall break forth into singing."* All of it done to express a deep devotion to the One true God who had saved me and blessed me.

It was precisely a year after that prophetic word that I, and a few other Christian musicians, were playing and singing in a convalescent hospital on a Sunday afternoon for a handful of elderly folks that just wanted to worship God. They sang, they clapped as we all worshiped God together. It was beautiful and the beginning of something that has been a mainstay in my ministry for over 40 years. Isaiah 55:12 became a "life – verse" for me.

Do you have one? Has someone spoken a promise of God over your life? Have you found a verse in the Scriptures that exactly fits who you are and what you do? Trust me, there is at least one for you. Look into His living word and allow the Holy Spirit to speak to you with promise and hope. You'll forever be grateful and amazed!

"For all the promises of God in Him are Yes, and in Him Amen, to the glory of God through us." (2 Corinthian 1:20)

RON KENOLY – MENTOR'S FROM AFAR / IMPACT FOR A LIFETIME

1983

HAVE YOU EVER HEARD OF the term: "a mentor from afar?" Do you have one? It simply means that someone who is at a distance from you has had an impact on your life. It is sometimes true that the mentor didn't know you very well and/or perhaps didn't know you at all. But, as you watched them from a distance, from afar, you gained knowledge and insight about certain things in life from them.

Such is the case for a few men in my life as well. If I were to name them it is simple; The late Pastor Chuck Smith of Calvary Chapel Costa Mesa. He was a mentor to many! Another would certainly be pastor Damian Kyle of Calvary Chapel Modesto. Those men associated with the movement are two at the top of my list. Terry and

Dwain Clark would also find themselves there because of their basic approach to worship leading. Keep it simple, don't bring attention to yourself and always point the worshiper to Jesus. They had a profound impact on my life from afar. But one other that needs a mention is a man named Ron Kenoly. Have you ever heard the name?

If you've ever enjoyed worship songs published by Integrity Music you may have sung his songs or even heard him singing without knowing it. Let me tell you how we met.

It was the spring of 1981. I was living in Oakland at the time and had just started going to church regularly whenever my work schedule allowed it. This small building on Foothill Boulevard was called "Faith Fellowship" and could hold maybe 75 people if every chair was filled. The mid-week services were lightly attended but powerful evenings of worship and study. It was there, in that small family of God seekers that I was introduced to Ron. He and a few others were always there on Wednesday nights leading the church in worship. Ron had been a worship leader for many years. His "Lou Rawls" type of voice and his passion for Jesus were enjoyed by many. After a few months of attending, I became curious about being involved musically. Musicians have a habit of doing so. I would hang around the piano after service and start a conversation with the various musicians. In my heart of hearts, I was still very self focused and saw playing worship music as just another extension of a "stage" for me to show off my skills. Boy did I have much to learn. It was that "old pattern" of playing and singing in front of people rising to the surface. Dick Mills had not yet spoken the promise of God over my life, and I was extremely young in my faith. (Dick Mills- previous chapter) For reasons to this day that I'm still unclear about the piano player suggested I come early the next Wednesday and bring my bass guitar with the possibility of assisting for one service. So, I did but what happened that night has changed me forever. What I witnessed that night has also altered my perspective of playing and singing in front of people for God's glory forever!

The Church service would begin at 7:00 pm. I showed up about 5:45. A few cars were in the parking lot, the doors were open, but no one was visible inside the sanctuary. I walked down the center isle and whispered "hello …, anyone here?" Setting my bass down I headed toward a side room that seemed to invite me to enter. As I opened the door the scene overwhelmed me. There, on their knees, and some on their faces before God was every musician and singer. Their whispers of worship, tears of joy, pain and cries for mercy struck deep in my heart! I found myself joining them immediately. In the center of that group, leading the way was Ron Kenoly. In that moment there was no thought of personal accolades for a talent displayed. In that moment there was no thought of chords and melody that might sound good. It was all about Jesus.

In that moment, through Ron and through those servants without one word spoken directly to me God taught me a lifelong principle. Whatever we do publicly in front of people that may bring God glory is only the result of the private relationship we have with Him. A successful and effective public ministry can only be the by-product of deep private devotion to God. In other words, it's what Jesus referred to in His teaching to His disciples written in the Gospel of John, chapter 15 and verse 5 when He said; "*I am the vine, you are the branches. He who abides in Me, and I in him, bears much fruit; for without Me you can do nothing.*" Men and women can do many things. But we can't do anything that is meaningful in the Kingdom of God and pleasing to the heart of God without the presence of the living God working through us. That is what they were asking for that night! For God to be glorified through their lives as they worshipped and lead people in worship! And that is what is to be asked for every time and everywhere we serve the Lord in any way.

Fast forward many years later to Lodi, California and another small church called Faith Fellowship. (Remember Ken Poore and Lodi, C.A. see above) Ron, his wife and children would one day come and stay in my home in Lodi while ministering at my local church. That up-close-and-personal time with him only cemented the things he had taught me from afar earlier in life. It was truly a blessed evening of song and worship. Ron's career as a popular recording artist and worship leader were growing. Integrity Music signed him for some projects and those records area still available for listening and enjoyment today.

However, today as you read this section and whenever a church service is about to begin here at Calvary Chapel Valley Springs, in a small room to the side of the platform you will find a few God seeking individual's. It is there amidst the whispers of worship, tears of joy, pain and cries for mercy that you will find us. Asking God to move in the moments that will follow as the body of Christ gathers. Mentor's from afar can greatly impact your life and walk with Christ. Do you have one? If not I encourage you to do so and allow the Lord to use that individual to help you live and learn and as you learn to live in even a greater appreciation for the grace of Go in your life.

DON LEVI – NEVER
TRY TO BOX GOD

1984 - 1987

WHAT IS IT ABOUT US human beings that we often try to put the living God into a box that fits our perception of who He is and what He does? Perhaps this chapter will help you grasp things differently, I hope.

During those first years after re-committing my life to Christ, and working for Lucky Stores, I was transferred to Lodi, California from the Bay Area. That event came after much earnest prayer. The issue for me at the time was that I didn't want to raise a family in the same area I had grown up. The streets of Oakland, the depressed lifestyle of rebellion against God had left its mark on me. It was a clouded perspective and one that I have grown out of. But back then, I wanted more for my children and believed it meant getting out of "dodge!" But the truth is that you can raise a Godly household anywhere if the parents are Godly people. I had yet to learn that truth.

So, after many written requests, loads of people praying and the favor of God, Lucky Stores transferred me from San Leandro to Lodi. Wow, what a ride. But it would be there, in Lodi, that I would learn a very big lesson about God's servants, God's ways and the possible traps of thinking that God works most with only one group of people over another. It's called denominationalism thinking. Many of the great Christian Churches that operate within their own denominational rules were, in their origins, wonderful fresh moves of God for their time. Yet, to think that God would restrict Himself to operate and bless one denomination over another is not founded in biblical truth.

Having previously re-educated my life to Christ in a "Four Square Gospel" church I immediately looked for one once I settled in Lodi. Faith Fellowship was a quaint little church of about 60 to 70 people. Many of its congregation were elderly and certainly older than me. Age has its benefits. Wisdom can be one of them and God knew I needed to be surrounded by wise men. One of which was a man named Don Levi. Don, with his wife Dolores, was the pastor of the church. His testimony is one that needs sharing because it can broaden anyone's spiritual horizons and keep one from the traps of denominational thinking. Let me explain.

When I first met Pastor Don Levi (pronounced – Le-vee) I was told that he came from a Jewish up-bringing. With a last name like "Levi" its no wonder. As he had told me, his parents weren't necessarily devout, but they did practice Judaism. The Sabbath, the Torah, the festivals, and observances were all a part of his life growing up as a young boy. But after leaving home and finishing college Don met Dolores. Dolores had come from a strictly Methodist family. She had been raised in the tenants of Methodism and was devout but her love for Don was deep. His love for her was equally deep and so only one thing would do. He would need to leave Judaism and accept the Methodist practices of worship. After all, it would be the same God that he, as a Jew and Dolores would be worshiping, right? But, it would be there in that Methodist church in Lodi that Don would come to accept Jesus Christ as his Savior. Amazing grace!

Once married, they attended the Lodi Methodist Church for some 20 years or more. They both worked as educators, raised a family, were regular church goer's and settled into a lovely home in the center of town. By the time their children had finished high school it was the late 1960's and the Jesus movement was in full swing. The Spirit of God had plans for the Levi's! Plans that they knew nothing about at the time but would begin to unfold by accepting an invitation to a prayer meeting. A very special prayer meeting.

As I said, the Jesus movement was in full swing in the late 1960's. Even though many people considered themselves Christians there was a deep hunger for more of the life of Christ. Being a pew-warmer was not enough. It never is. God wanted more than just church attendance from His children. He was seeking a revived heart. Thus, the Holy Spirit was moving upon broken lives, churched and un-churched alike were experiencing an awakening of the soul and its need for repentance and forgiveness. Into that environment, Don was invited to a Charismatic prayer meeting at a Catholic Church. Yep, you heard that right. A Catholic Charismatic prayer meeting. I had never heard of such a thing until I met Don. As he began attending the meetings something happened. On one such evening he was "filled, or baptized with the Spirit!" Suddenly, a fresh and new relationship with Jesus Christ had been awakened in him. He began to live and experience some of the giftings of the Spirit. Speaking in tongues, words of wisdom and knowledge, miracles, and healings. The word of God came alive to him as never before and there was change. We call it revival!

So, the Lodi Methodist Church was no longer feeding their hungry souls causing Don and Dolores to start attending elsewhere, but where? They chose to try Century Assembly of God (CAG). There at CAG Don was introduced to ministry. He began as a Sunday School teacher helping young children in the church learn about the gospel of Jesus Christ and the Jesus of that gospel. It wasn't long before his gifts as a teacher were recognized by the leadership, and he was invited to be a leader of a men's group. The roadmap for Don was clearly being laid as one day the pastor called him into his office. He explained that there was a small "Four-Square Gospel" church a few blocks away that had lost its pastor. The district superintendent for the ministry had contacted the Assembly of God pastor and wanted to meet Don and talk with him. It was during that meeting that God placed a call on Don's life to enter pastoral ministry. His obedience changed my life forever. It was at Faith Fellowship of the Four Square Gospel that Don, Dolores and I first met.

We should all be able to see that you can't box God into a corner. His ways are higher than our ways. He doesn't operate in a "fixed" un-flexible cold and lifeless environment. He is not restricted to work only in certain denominations. He will usher change into any and every environment to accomplish His purposes.

How else can you explain that God would take a Jewish child, make him a Methodist congregant to save him.

Then baptize him with the Holy Spirit in a Catholic charismatic meeting, groom him for service during a short tenure at an Assembly of God church to then place him as a under shepherd and senior pastor in the midst of a needy fellowship of a Four Square Gospel denomination? Explain that to me please? You can't! Because it's a God thing. Don't try to box God in denominationally or otherwise.

Just let Him work in and through your life. Don was the first man who would believe that God had a similar call upon my life. As battered torn and tarnished as my life was compared to his he could see possibilities for my life in serving God! It would be under Don's ministry that I would grow as a husband, father and fledgling worship leader. It would be in that little fellowship that I would experience deep loss and great love. All because God had his sights on a man named Don Levi. A man that would not try to place God in a box himself! I will always be grateful to God for Don. He's in heaven as I write this. And I'll bet he's greeting everyone with a variety of denominational backgrounds and histories into the pearly gates and smiling the whole time.

THE ELDER / THE MEMORIAL – A COMPACT COMPASSION

1988

THIS IS A DIFFICULT QUESTION because it's a difficult fact but it must be asked. Have you ever lost someone you love unexpectedly to death? Perhaps even more difficult is the question, have you ever lost a child unexpectedly? In either case I grieve with you and in the later case I especially empathize with you today. In my case I lost a son, his name is Daniel. He's in heaven as I'm writing this. He was a precious six-year-old boy when God chose to take him home. I'll share a little bit of the experience with you.

The phone call came while I was at work in Lucky Stores in Jackson, CA. The hospital nurse asked me to confirm my name and informed me that there had been an accident and my son Daniel was in the hospital. She wanted me to come to the hospital immediately. I questioned her about his condition and asked; " ...is he ok?" Her answer was calm and to the point: " ...he's being cared for and we will update you as soon as you get here!" I later came to understand that her answer was hospital protocol designed to keep a parent safe and calm while driving to the destination. There was nothing untrue about her answer and I'm grateful for it.

As I rushed into the waiting area I was met with professionals that surrounded me, informed me that Daniel had passed away and then led me into a room to identify the body. As I walked into the room where my six year old son's body lay I could not believe my eyes. To this day it is surreal but true, he was gone. God had called him home. Why then? I don't know. But there is a glimpse of the possibility in scripture. Isaiah tells us that; *"The righteous perishes, And no man takes it to heart; Merciful men are taken away, While no one considers That the righteous is taken away from evil."(Is.57:1)* Daniel had declared his faith in Christ at a very young age and therefore, the Bible says that in God's eyes, because of the blood of Jesus he was righteous. Perhaps the Lord wanted to "take Daniel away" from an evil that was coming. I'll find out when I see him in heaven. (Smile). Here is what happened that day.

He and another friend had been riding their bikes in a small track of homes. A seemly safe enough area to allow a six year old and his friend to ride. When he decided to cross a larger street he pulled right out in front of a young man's vehicle. There was nothing the young man could do except slam on the breaks. The impact knocked Daniel unconscious. When the Paramedics arrived on the sceen, he had a pulse and they tried feverishly to save him. A helicopter was called in, they med-i-flighted him to Dameron Hospital in Stockton with the intent to perform lifesaving surgery but his time had come. God whispered to him to come home and in that flight, he breathed his last breath. The hospital classified him as D.O.A. Dead on arrival.

There is a sad statistic that exists today. Families that experience the death of child are high in divorce rates. I, unfortunately, joined that statistic and was forced to navigate through a divorce as well. Truly it was one of the most painful times in my life. I'm sure you might agree. But, no matter how deep your grief, compassion from others can leave a lasting impression upon your heart. This is where the "Elder" comes in. Let me explain.

At Daniel's "Celebration of Life" there were many relatives and friends. Faith Fellowship of Lodi had agreed to let us hold the service there. Don Levi, the pastor, officiated and carried these hurting parents through the moments of closure. One thing that I need to include here is, that it had been many months since I had been in church. Even before the accident I had become a bit distant to church going. After his passing the turmoil and grief at home had taken its toll. In my confusion, I'd stopped attending and worshiping with others for quite a while. Although there was an occasional call asking me if things were ok I'd chosen to isolate. Always a bad choice for any Christian.

Proverbs 18:1, tells us that: " ...A man who isolates himself seeks his own desire; He rages against all wise judgment." I was certainly not being wise and as far as my own desires, well lets just say they weren't necessarily heavenly.

So there I was, now facing folks that had known me but hadn't seen me for quite some time. They were there to offer their condolences and help if they could. As the scriptures says;

"...that we may be able to comfort those who are in any trouble, with the comfort with which we ourselves are comforted by God." (1 Corinthians 1:4) They were there to comfort us. Sweet is the body of Christ. And as hard and as difficult as those days and months were there is something else true in the life of all who have submitted their lives to the hand of the living God.

In all loss there is the opportunity for gain. In tragedy there is the offer of triumph, in brokenness there can be healing and such is the case with Daniel's passing. Let me also share some of that experience with you now.

Much of Daniel's Celebration of Life is a blur but there is one person and moment that stands out. The circumstance is still very clear. As I was leaving the memorial that afternoon a very precious man walked up to me whom I had known as an elder in the church. I don't remember his name today and for that I am sorry. That is why I'm calling him: "The Elder!" His very presence at that moment made me think I needed to explain why I hadn't been to church in so long. I was wrong. That was the last thing on his mind. All he did was open his arms and hug me! I wept! We stood in that embrace silent! Wiping my eyes I stepped back and tried to apologize for being "out of fellowship". His words were an expression of compact compassion that I'll never forget. He said: " ...Art you haven't been out of fellowship you just haven't been to church. Your never out of fellowship with Jesus. He's been there the whole time. Don't confuse the two. I love you and come when you can we'll be here!"

God used this very special man to make two things very real to me there and then. First, it became clear that as a professing Christian my worth was not measured in church attendance or church activities. Somehow I became immediately aware of a deeper reality. God's people are what constitute the church and not the building. In the New Testament, Jesus calls the church His bride and one day the Groom will return to retrieve her. He won't be taking any buildings with him will He? After all, there is something about mansions in the heaven already waiting for those that enter. Ever since that conversation I have viewed those things differently.

Secondly, his words tattooed a fact about Christ's closeness to the heart of His child into my mind. A verse in the Bible describes how personal to me that truth had become. It goes like this: "For I am persuaded that neither death nor life, nor angels nor principalities nor powers, nor things present nor things to come, nor height nor depth, nor any other created thing, shall be able to separate us from the love of God which is in Christ Jesus our Lord." (Romans 8:38-39)

The Lord had not left me, I was simply distancing myself from His presence. The Lord had not separated Himself from me, He remained faithful even when I was not. I may have taken my eyes off of Him, but never did He take His eye off of me.

May I ask you about the hardship or tragedy you are facing today? Is it small, large or somewhere in between?

Has there been a tendency to isolate yourself from others and ignore the help and comfort of Almighty God? Allow me to use this very personal experience of mine to encourage you about the truth of God, His word and His people.

He will never leave you nor forsake you. He is always near to the broken hearted, knocking on the door of a heart and wanting to come in and abide. Why not just let Him? You'll be amazed at the results. Remember, He will often use another person in your life path as His hands, His arms and His ear to comfort and hold you in times of hardship. We will call it compact compassion.

LUCKY'S MEAT SUPERVISOR.
– A TOOL IN THE HAND

1987

Currently we find ourselves placing an acronym on everything, don't we? Consider the fact that: "What Would Jesus Do" has become WWJD. For Your Information has been transformed into F.Y.I. The designation for the Joint Chiefs Section of Operations is reduced to J.C.S.O. and a most familiar one would be our own proud acronym of USA which needs no explanation in this chapter except perhaps for those of the cancel culture. (Smile)

With acronyms in mind I have decided to place one more on a very unique person. He was short lived in my life but very instrumental in various ways. In fact I would go on record as saying that he was a "tool in the hand of God!" We will call him L.M.S. which will stand for Lucky's Meat Supervisor. My original supervisor in the

Bay Area was a man named Ben Tiapon (see previous chapter) but as I transferred out to the San Joaquin Valley that all changed.

Meat supervisors were always coming and going in the grocery business. Because there were so many of them I can not remember LMS's name while I worked in the Lodi area but, he was a very important man. I'll explain.

By the winter of 1987 I had been bouncing around from one store to another in order to pick up my 40 hours as a journeyman and that aggravated me greatly. After all, I had left the Bay Area with almost 3 years of seniority. (That is not much anywhere let alone in chain store) In my uneducated opinion I had believed it would be enough seniority to land me a sweet, 9 to 5, Monday through Friday position somewhere close to home, right? The answer to that question in the grocery business is: "no way!" There is no such thing for a butcher in a chain store environment. In fact, when I applied to move from San Leandro, I had been told that I would lose all my seniority for the first six months of transfer. It was a gamble that I was willing to make at the time. But I quickly became aggravated about moving around after the 6 months had come and gone.

As the months turned into years, each time I would see my L.M.S. I would greet him with a hello, ask how he was and then ask the million dollar question. "When are you going to give me a home store with a fixed schedule?" He would say things like: " ...I'll see what I can do ...". But his real answer often came wrapped up in the next schedule that had me traveling once again. Funny isn't it? But that's when it happened.

One day he came in and said: " ...Ok Art, I'm moving you to a home store and after a short period of time you'll probably have a fixed schedule!" I was overwhelmed with joy at first. "Ok great I said, where too?" His answer floored me: "Jackson." Jackson? Did he forget that I was living in Lodi? Did he not remember it was going to be an hour drive each way each day? No, he didn't forget!

I'm the one who had forgotten that God answers prayer according to His purposes and not ours. It's amazing to me how quick I was, as a young Christian, to complain about the way God had just answered my long-awaited prayer! Have you ever reacted with a complaint to the way God answered a prayer in your life? Did you ever say something like: " ...oh thanks God but I didn't want you to answer it that way ...!" If you have then you now realize you are not alone.

The rest of the story goes like this. For quite a few months prior to my son Daniel's accidental death, (see previous chapter) I had become a bit disillusioned with church life and Christianity in general. As I have explained earlier in this book, turmoil at home, a difficult work schedule and a bad attitude all gave way to bad thinking. Going to church or spending time with other Christians became something I did not do regularly or very often at all. But here are some important insights. After Daniel's death, which tragically led to a divorce and the hardships that followed, my transfer as a meat cutter in Jackson became even more important. Here is why.

Having that responsibility to fulfill each week was, by God's grace, something that kept me man on track. I was fighting many failed aspirations as a young man. An immature and unbiblical perspective of Christianity had led me to believe that life should be a "Jesus and happily ever after" story. Death, divorce, and a sense of personal failure had placed real things on the scales of my life. I remember saying things like; "God, where are you?" And things like; "Jesus, I don't understand why this is happening?" And although it was an emotionally crushing time for me, interestingly enough my relationship with the Lord actually began to deepen.

The apostle Peter tells us that: "...*the genuineness of your faith, being much more precious than gold that perishes, though it is tested by fire, may be found to praise, honor and glory at the revelation of Jesus Christ.*" (1 Peter 1:7) In other words, I was beginning to learn what Peter meant about hardships mixed with a tested faith in Christ being the things that cause us to grow and mature.

What I did not realize at the time of my transfer was that God was looking ahead in time. As the Bible declares; "…For the LORD will go before you, And the God of Israel will be your rear guard." (Is.52:12). He was going ahead of me because of what was coming against me down the road.

The pain of a failed marriage, loosing one son to death and my other son due to custody issues was overwhelming. What I needed were brothers in Christ. What I needed was to remain being taught the word of God. What I needed was a pastor and a church family. But the respectful thing to do was to leave Faith Fellowship in Lodi and look for a new one. Allow others to go on with their own lives while I start over somewhere else. This is where Jackson and my Lucky's Supervisor place as a tool in God's hand becomes clearer.

They say that hindsight is 20-20. I will attest to that. The very place that I complained about being transferred to inevitably became a heaven and refuge in a time of trouble. The Jackson store, a church in the city itself, a God seeking new pastor and a new church family all became instruments that God used to heal and restore me. Eventually the hurts and failures were replaced with the joy of the Lord and the hope found in His word. The transfer happened in 1987 and as I write today it is 2021. I live 15 minutes away and truly Jackson was God's will for my life and my LMS was simply a tool in God's hand.

Is there a person being a "tool in the hands of God" in your life today? Are there moves and circumstances that seem to make no sense at all? If you are His child, then just wait. We are told that He *"...works all things together for the good, to them that love God, to them called according to His purpose."* (Romans 8:28). So, ask God to meet you and calm you. Stop the screaming or complaining and trust that HE is working out something for you that you will understand much better in hindsight! Its called "trust!" Listen to what Solomon tells us in his book of wisdom known as Proverbs, chapter 3, verses 5 and 6: "Trust in the LORD with all your heart, And lean not on your own understanding; In all your ways acknowledge Him, And He shall direct your paths." Let it be so for you today. Trust the Hand of God that is guiding the tool being used to direct your life.

ED GALLOWAY – A LESSON IN HUMILITY

1989

Webster's Dictionary defines "humility" as being: "freedom from pride or arrogance." Arrogance was always something that I thought other people had, not me! (You can laugh now if you'd like). But the truth of the matter is that every human being must deal with the element of pride and/or arrogance in their heart at some point in life and perhaps many times as well. In my case it came at the expense of someone else delivering the truth bomb. All the sudden I knew I was guilty! Let's take a moment to consider why.

Ed Galloway was a good Meat Department manager, a fair boss, and a man that ended up as my friend and eventually a fellow brother in the Lord. He has gone home to heaven as I write this memoir, but I first met Ed at the Lodi Lucky's Store that I was transferred too in

1983. It was a new store opening and they were willing to take on new butchers. As soon as the new business died down, I was put on the road traveling to find my forty hours each week. The experience of working for and with Ed for those first months was classic. He was a dedicated manager with a method of doing things that could not be altered, especially by the new kid on the butcher block. (Pun intended)

As life would have it and as God would order it, years later I would come to work for Ed again in the Jackson store. (See: L.M.S. tool in the hand). But this time there would be a very important lesson to learn from him. I'll explain. In a grocery store meat department, there is always a "pecking" order of sorts. It usually surfaces in multiple ways. A meat cutter's seniority will play a part in the order but a person's experience and know how plays even a greater part. For instance, if you've been cutting meat for ten years but don't work well with the team or are un-teachable about new department protocols then you will be low in the pecking order. Ten years or not. Someone with less time will rise above you because they work well and are willing to learn new ways of doing the same thing. This is where I come in.

I had been trained in the Bay Area and a different environment than the Central Valley. At a ripe young age in my early 30's I also believed myself to have a certain accumulative knowledge. That being said, there were some work habits that I had picked up that would not serve me well.

It all started with a simple night shift protocol. Each meat cutter working the night shift was responsible to clean a large drain trap located in the center of the floor. Much of the day's cutting waste would end up in this trap after the room was hosed down and sanitized. It was never a real pleasant duty but certainly not hard.

A person might get away with not cleaning the trap one night and no one would know unless they lifted the drain cover and looked! But the meat cutter working the next night shift would know that they were facing two days of meat trash and not one! Anytime I chose to ignore the trap until the next night I thought I was within my rights sense I'm the one who will clean it the next night. Right? Wrong! Remember what I said about Ed's methods of doing things that could not be altered? Well, it all came to a head after a few weeks of me ignoring my duties and being discovered.

Now, lets step back for a moment and take something else into consideration. Remember my story about Hume Lake? (See Ken Poore). Well, the short of it is that I was supposed to be the "Christian" in the shop. Always telling the other meat cutters about God, and how wonderful it is to be a Christian. I would share my love for the Bible and the truth's that are in it. At times I was even passing judgment on certain language used or certain ideas expressed.

There is a verse in Colossians 3 and verse 23 that says; "whatever you do, do as unto the Lord!" What that means is that wherever you are as a Christian you and I are to remember we represent Christ. We are to remember we are serving Christ in our homes, in our workplaces. When we do well Christ is honored. If we willfully do poorly Christ is mocked by those around us looking to find a fault or weakness. If we talk the talk but don't walk the walk we are, in effect, hypocritical. And that, my friend, is still one of the largest complaints by the unbeliever about the professing Christians today. The presence of hypocrisy in our witness is a sad thing and it breaks the heart of God.

So there I was, telling people how they should live but coming up real short in my willingness to follow orders and live right in the workplace myself. Ouch! It always hurts when you see your own sin running around on your feet!

I walked into work one day and was met with an invitation to step into the walk in refrigerator! As I opened the door, I was followed by all three of my work mates. Ed, as the manager, and two others. The co-workers were there as a witness to the fact that they had cleaned my trap many times. I had nothing to say when confronted except: "yes, I'd willfully ignored my duties!" To add to the problem, I had been warned. Weeks before I remember my co-workers mentioning things like: " …hey Phinney, don't forget to clean the trap tonight …". To which I would respond: " … sure thing!" So, this was the moment of truth.

As the conversation in the cooler continued, I was told that I would be placed on all night shift's for an indefinite period of time. That really hurt! It hurt my pride more than anything. It was a revelation about how proud and arrogant I had become. Thinking that any job in the department was below me! What arrogance. Thinking that I could choose when to obey my bosses' orders and when not too! Wow, what destructive pride! The bottom line is that I had forgotten about the Christ-like virtue of humility. A lesson in humility had become necessary! Ed and my co-workers became the instruments God used to teach me a much needed lesson.

Those were long nights. It was a long several weeks. Needless to say, that there were words each time I cleaned the trap at night! I could almost be heard talking to myself or thinking out loud as some call it. At first I would say things like: "why me God, they have faults too?" Then it turned into things like; "that was silly of you Phinney …". Eventually the appropriate words became; " …I'm sorry Lord, forgive me and help me be a better worker and witness!" Have you ever been there?

What do you do when you realize your own faults in some area of your home life or work place? Do you immediately want to blame someone else? Do you ever look for a way to justify your own wrongdoing? The old saying is true: When you point a finger at someone three point back at yourself. Here are some thoughts on humility from the Word of God.

- When pride comes, then comes shame; But with the humble is wisdom. (Proverbs 11:2)
- Better to be of a humble spirit with the lowly, than to divide the spoil with the proud. (Proverbs 16:19)
- A man's pride will bring him low, But the humble in spirit will retain honor. (Proverbs 29:23)

Oh my … that was a very humiliating lesson but one most needed at the time. One that I have not forgotten and a lesson that continues to bear fruit in my life today. Here is the take away for me. God used Ed Galloway to be His servant and teach another one of His servants about Himself and the virtue of humility.

Who is God using to teach you about humility in your life today? Whoever it might be try to remember they are there for your good and His glory!

A DENOMINATIONAL PASTOR ... WORDS THAT CUT AND YET, RE-DIRECT

1992

LET ME START THIS SECTION with an apology for the history lesson you are about to hear. I trust that you will appreciate it a bit further down the road. We will see. As the title of this chapter mentions I want to explain a little bit about Denominational Christianity.

Christian Denominations are an interesting thing. The first such denomination that remains in place to this day is the Catholic Church. This was the single most prominent Denomination until around the 1400's and the Reformation. At which point Christianity became divided into two main groups. Eastern and Western theology. From these two groups emerged six branches. They are: Catholicism, Protestantism, Eastern Orthodoxy, Anglicanism, Oriental Orthodoxy, and

Assyrians. Restorationism is sometimes considered the seventh branch. The major Protestant denominational families are: Adventist, Baptists, Congregationalists, Lutherans, Methodist, Pentecostals and Presbyterians.

Each of these branches have a set of codes and/or rules, hopefully Biblical, by which the entire Denomination operates and is in submission too. It's a huge subject all by itself. One that we will not tackle here.

But I share this with you to help you see that these codes and rules don't always allow room for change. In other words, what was once a framework of rules guiding various Christian movements to grow and thrive also became walls to high for some to climb. Hurdles that would prevent others from reaching their God appointment places in life. Let me try to bring those lofty statements down to earth with a personal explanation.

When I first re-dedicated my life to Christ in 1980, I attended a church that was part of the Pentecostal (see previous list) Denominations. It was within that framework that I grew closer to Jesus and His body, the church. As those first years rolled by I was completely content to continue with that denomination. It was flourishing and so was I. There seemed to be an anointing within that church sect that I agreed with. And I thoroughly enjoyed the Lord. Let us not forget that these years were also the years of the Jesus Movement and there was revival in the air everywhere! So much for God operating more powerfully in one group over another. (smile)

It was around the six year mark that tragedy challenged my faith and changed my life. As I have stated earlier in this book, it all started with the loss of my oldest son at six year old son to a car accident. (See The Elder / Compact Compassion) As I've already explained, that led to my first marriage dissolving, loosing most of my contact with my younger son and ultimately some confusion about what God had called me to do in life. You see, up until that time I had begun to think that the Lord wanted to place me in ministry. Although I was a butcher for Lucky Stores, I was now helping teach Sunday School and was growing as an occasional worship leader in my church.

It is not abnormal for someone radically saved to believe they're being called into full time service for God. Examples of such things were all around me at the time. Keith Green and the Last Days Ministries, Mike MacIntosh and Horizon Christian Fellowship, Greg Lourie with his Harvest Crusades, and many others. These were men who had once walked a destructive secular road but were now serving the Lord in powerful ways. I was beginning to entertain and hope for similar things when pain, suffering, and yes, altered circumstances knocked hard on my front door! But there is a powerful principle here that must be observed.

It comes to us through the account of Moses and the children of Israel. He was called to lead them out of Egypt, but he was not sent to do that work until much later in his life. Forty years of trial and hardship to be exact. It was there that Moses leaned to care for sheep in the desert. It is a lesson that I would learn also. The calling and the sending are often different! This is where a denominational pastor and his important words come in.

I had been transferred to the Jackson, Lucky Store. I was now a single man living in San Andreas, CA. I had visited a few churches looking for a new church home but was unsettled. I had so hoped God could use my life and testimony to further the good news of the Gospel. But right now, I was very broken, confused, and unsure of my future service to God. With that as a background allow me to share a story.

One sunny afternoon I was driving home from work and decided to drop into a local denominational church that I had yet to visit. My hope was that the pastor, or a leader, would be there to counsel and comfort me about my tragic situation and lost expectations for ministry. What happened next was very unexpected.

The sunlight broke through the sanctuary windows as I entered. It was surreal. I sensed the presence of God. The Bible tells that: " …The LORD is near to those who have a broken heart and saves such as have a contrite spirit." (Psalm 34:18). So, it wasn't the beauty of the sanctuary room but rather the brokenness of the man entering the room that brought His presence that day. As I knocked on the office door that was ajar, I was welcomed by the pastor, sitting at his desk. He offered me a seat and asked how he might help me.

As I explained myself and gave him details about my son's death, my divorce, and my remaining desire to serve God in ministry he listened intently. But when I was finished his response went something like this; " …you can serve the Lord here in some ways, but you'll *never be ordained into ministry* because our denominational rules do not allow it." He was being honest, sensitive, and clear. I respected him for it. But by those same words I was being broken further and crushed. His words had cut like a knife! Never being ordained into ministry was what I walked out of that church with that day. It seemed I had been denied my opportunity for ministry because of life's circumstance.

The truth of the moment was that I had misplaced my hope. I had placed my hope in something called ministry, when the Bible clearly reminds us to place our hope in God alone. He will never let us down. He will never let you down. Where is your hope today? Is it in a relationship, a carrier, a circumstance? David's words are so spot on for us all: " ...Why are you cast down, O my soul? And why are you disquieted within me? Hope in God ..." (Ps. 42:5)

Someone once said that when God closes one door, He always opens a window. When the apostle Paul was denied permission to preach it was a shock! We read in Acts 16:6: " ...they were forbidden by the Holy Spirit to preach the word in Asia."

One night after being forbidden by the Holy Spirit to go to Asia, Paul had a vision. In that vision he saw a man calling out to him and saying: *"Come over to Macedonia and help us."* Now after he had seen the vision, immediately he and Luke sought to go to Macedonia, *"...concluding that the Lord had called us to preach the gospel to them."* (Acts 16:9-10) When we consider the illogic perspective of that circumstance we are forced to ask the question: " ...why would the Holy Spirit not want someone (Paul) to preach the Gospel in Asia?" Answer. Because He, the Holy Spirit, had something else in mind for Paul to do. He had a different plan for Paul than the one Paul had for himself. In short, Paul was re-directed in ministry and life by a denial. The same has become true for me. God used those cutting words from a sincere denominational pastor to re-direct my life. I began wondering what kind of church I would find and eventually call home? That's when it happened. A co-worker invited me to a new-year's eve gathering at a nearby "non-denominational" church called, Warehouse Ministries. It was a Calvary Chapel affiliate. I decided to go, why not?

As I entered the little makeshift rugged sanctuary that night there was no sunlight coming through windows. There was no surreal sense of the presence of God. But there was a loving body of believer's ready to wrap their arms around me and accept me as I was. I eventually came to find a pastor, George Stathos, who welcomed my zeal and desires for ministry. In the years that followed he would teach me and wait patiently while God matured me and healed my brokenness. It would be there at Warehouse Ministries, Jackson, that God brought Sherry into my life. She would become my beloved wife. That little country non-denominational church would witness God mending two lives and binding them together. That fellowship was a conduit for God's grace and would eventually ordain me into ministry to serve.

As I close, I will say that a denominational church or rule can be a very good thing. Many of the denominations that exists today have thriving fellowships. I thank God for the entirety of His body that is expressed through denominational and non-denominational churches. Yet, I'm especially thankful that the Lord has called me into the family of Calvary Chapel churches.

It just so happened that with this man it was a denominational rule that brought words that cut and yet re-directed my life. It's so important to simply keep our eyes on Jesus and our hope in Him alone.

GEORGE STATHOS –
TANGIBLE GRACE

1988-1996

Let's start with idea's that require some thinking to understand and envision. For instance, have you ever chased a dream? It's a phrase shaped in a metaphor that describes a person's pursuit of a hope they have in life. You can't literally chase a dream, but we all know what it means. Or, have you ever reached for the sky? Again, it's a statement that portrays a person working hard to reach a faraway a goal. Most of us have an idea of what those statements mean. But if I wanted to paint you a picture of a phrase called tangible grace, I would begin with a name. That name would be George Stathos.

So, let's define the phrase "Tangible Grace"! The essential meaning of tangible according to Webster's Dictionary is as follows; (1): easily seen or recognized and (2): able to be touched or felt. The essential meaning of grace according to the New Testament is; "un-merited favor." The word, "grace", in both testaments of the Bible, is a word that appears often. It has various applications, but it has that one central definition of un-merited favor. Thus, for our purposes here, tangible grace would be un-merited favor toward others that is easily seen and felt by those upon whom it is given.

George Stathos is a dear friend, a devoted brother in Christ and was for many years a pastor to me and my family. He was known to always give favor to those when they may not have warranted it. You could recognize lives that his counsel and care had affected by the fact that they had touched and felt God's grace through George's life as their pastor. I call that tangible grace. This is how we met.

It started one New Year's Eve in 1988. I had been invited to this little church in Jackson that was gathering for an evening of fellowship and prayer to bring in the new year. It's intimidating to go into a new church where you don't know anyone. Bruce, the assistant store manager for Lucky's where I was currently a meat cutter, had told me about this church event and encouraged me to try it out. Having just moved to San Andreas, near Jackson and being unsettled in a church home yet I decided to go.

When I entered the cozy make-shift sanctuary I was immediately greeted with a handshake and a warm piercing smile. Unknown to me at the time it was pastor George welcoming me to the event. I was introduced to a few new faces and names and then eventually found Bruce. Once the festivities began all things seemed to become comfortable and fun. I was among the family of God.

As mentioned earlier in this book I was in need of many things! My world had recently been rocked by the death of one son and an un-preventable divorce. As a young Christian, at age 35, I wasn't sure how I'd fit into new settings. The few houses of worship that I had previously visited during this season of my life had left me feeling out of place and alone. Have you ever felt all alone in a church full of people? It's a strange feeling for sure. My job as a meat cutter was familiar to me but going home to an empty apartment and new surroundings was always difficult. Many evenings were spent pouring out the pain in my heart to the Lord. I really wasn't sure about my future with the family of God. That new years eve gathering had succeeded in placing a new hope in my heart. Perhaps I would try this church for a while and see what God had for me.

The following Sunday morning I returned to the building where the new years eve event had taken place. I found myself visiting Warehouse Ministries Jackson. The small industrial building turned into a-church sanctuary was a new concept for me. There were about 80 folding chairs set out and the atmosphere was delightful. Friendly faces greeted me as I came in the door and looking for a seat I decided on one about in the middle back left.

I remember someone stepping up to a microphone and extending a verbal welcome to the small crowd. Then he invited us to join him in an opening prayer. Next, the worship team took over leading the fellowship in songs. They lead us in festive, celebratory, and worshipful songs. After a few announcements about things happening in and around the church a dark-haired young man took center platform and sat at the podium. His smile, warm tone and passionate love for God was striking. It was the same man who had welcomed me earlier that week. They called him pastor George.

As we opened the Bible that morning, pastor George taught the passage in a way that was very new and insightful to me. He would read a verse, explain it, expound upon it and then apply it to his life. My previous sermon experiences had been spent listening to "topical" messages. This was a new and engaging way to study the bible. Book by book, chapter by chapter and verse by verse. Afterwards, I approached pastor George and thanked him for the message. I re-introduced myself to him and shared some of my painful circumstances. I'm sure I implied I would be making this church my new home. He listened and then offered to pray with me. He asked God to lead me in my decisions and guide me in my way. Gracious, very gracious. Tangible grace.

As the new year began and the weeks turned into months Warehouse Ministries became my home. By March of 1989 I was once more involved helping to teach children's Sunday School classes. It was such a joy to have a place to express my love for the Lord again. It was such a privilege to be trusted and accepted as a believer and not feel like I was under a microscope about my past. By Easter, events in the church opened the door for me to share some music and start serving as a worship leader for Sunday services. Amazing grace. Tangible grace.

Let's stop for a moment and re-visit the timeline of events. The New Year's Eve gathering was December 31st. Easter came in April the next year. December to April was less than 5 full months. Would you think that to be a very short time for a young man, new to a Christian fellowship, working through hard circumstances to be invited to start leading worship services? You would be right. This is another example of George's tangible grace. He would always assume the best in others until shown differently. That is grace. Tangible grace.

My story was my own, but I've come to understand that many broken individuals walk into church settings wanting to serve God. That is commonplace because the body of Christ should always be a place to heal and mend. But it is always wise to be patient and take some time before placing those same individuals in up-front ministries. It's prudent to let God work out the details of the testimony in a person's life before quickly placing them as a leader. Not George with me! He counseled me and discipled me all through those painful times. As he got to know me better, he trusted the Lord in me. As a result, I have learned from his example to do the same for others. Tangible grace.

Fast forward, for two years I became the designated worship leader at Jackson Warehouse Ministries'. Eventually I was ordained and brought on staff. I served there from April 1989 until I left for the School of Ministry in August of 1995. It was there at Warehouse Ministries that God began to bring into fruition things that I had only dreamed about. A restored life in many tangible ways. It was there that God brought Sherry into my life and my 5 stepdaughters. (Whom many of them are simply referred to as daughters). At this writing, we have celebrated 32 years of bliss, blessed marriage. With a blended family of five girls and one son we are watching many grandchildren grow into tremendous adults. It was my privilege to be mentored by George for 6 wonderful years.

Eventually the church in Jackson was renamed Calvary Chapel Pine Grove. One more by-product of God's tangible grace operating through His servant, George Stathos. When encountering the life of George Stathos, one will always recognize this. They will find what is easily seen and able to be touched and felt. The grace of God working though one of His servants. May we all learn and practice the value of tangible grace operating through our lives as well. Thank you, George!

RUSSEL THE BUSS DRIVER
– " ...DON'T WORRY,
THEY BE BACK ..."

1994-1995

HAVE YOU EVER RIDDEN IN a big yellow School Buss? The very mention of the word conjures up many a fond memory. Here are a few. As an elementary student singing with the Oakland City Boys Choir, I had the fun of riding from East Oakland down to the Lake Merritt area for rehearsals. As a student at King Jr. High School, also in Oakland, I rode in a school buss to our Band competitions. What fun that was. But there is one school buss situation especially important to share today. Let me begin with Russell. Russel was a school bus driver in Amador County Unified School District for many years. He was an African American and very well known or his southern drawl, his quick whit and kind heart. Each day he took care of many children while seeing to it that they were picked up and dropped off safely. This was no exception when it came to any of our daughters that rode the buss during their School years.

It was a short time after graduation that one of our girls had decided to move out and live on her own. To keep things in perspective we must remember that this is really their job. Its your children's job to grow and go! We raise them to send them into the world on their own! The challenge is learning to let go when they want to go even if we, as a parent, don't think they are ready. (Smile). Back to the story.

One day, soon after this same daughter had moved out, Sherry and I were shopping at the local grocery store. While shopping we ran into Russell. As we greeted him in the food isle we rejoiced to see his smiling face. He was always so cheerful and seemed to be full of the joy of the Lord. His conversation soon turned to a question about the well being of our girls. He remembered them well from the years before. As we began to express our concerns for the one that had moved out he listened intently. We went on and on into great detail, imagining all kinds of possible problems that could be occurring in her life. Clearly, we were worried and Russel could see it and hear it.

With what seemed to be the wisdom of the ages and the insight of a caring brother his response has stayed with us forever. Russel uttered a few words that left us at peace and turned out to be somewhat prophetic. In his jovial southern drawl he declared; *"...don't worry, they be back ... more trouble than what they left with!"* Now before you walk away from this story wondering what was the point, let me decipher that statement. What Russel was saying in his slang sort of way was this.

Sometimes, adult children in our lives that leave the nest prematurely can end up returning home because of circumstances beyond they're control. Sometimes those same adult children return home with various things and changes that took place in their life while they were away. Those things and changes can be conflicts, or situations or "problems" that must be confronted and dealt with right away! All taking place while that same adult child re-establishes residency again in your home. Another way of re-phrasing Russell's statement would be; "don't worry, they'll be back and when they come back there may very well be more things to deal with than when they left in the first place". Make sense to you?

In our life and in this daughter's life this was certainly true. When she finally returned home she had been married, given birth to two children, her husband had tragically died in an auto accident and she was now a single mom in much need of help. We welcomed her home and began to help her care for our first grandchildren. Those were formative years for Sherry and I. We depended so much upon the grace of God each day to teach us and lead us in how we were to help. Many lessons were learned about unconditional love. Many opportunities were given to express the love of God to our her as an adult, single mom in need of a helping hand.

My prayer for you as a parent, is that in your lifetime neither you or any of your children would have to experience that kind of hardship, pain or grief. But I know this that if so, God is able to *"...comfort the broken hearted and He is near to those of contrite spirit!"* (Ps. 34:18). Today, that same daughter is doing well. Her children are grown adults leading lives of their own.

If you are a concerned parent today and wondering about the safety and well being of a child that is out on their own, I understand. Perhaps when they left the communication wasn't the best. Perhaps there aren't a lot of phone calls and time spent filling in the gaps of what is going on in their life presently. Maybe you worry and wonder what to do about them. We parents have those things in common because once a parent always a parent.

But I would like to point you to something the apostle Paul said to Christians in the town of Philippi. Its found in the book of Philippians, the 4th Chapter and verses 6-7.

He said this; "Be anxious for nothing, but in everything by prayer and supplication, with thanksgiving, let your requests be made known to God; and the peace of God, which surpasses all understanding, will guard your hearts and minds through Christ Jesus."

Do you see it? Coming to God in prayer for your loved one and mixing that time of prayer with thanksgiving can change things. Most of all it will change you. The situation that you are concerned about may or may not change but God will change how you deal with it. He will give you a supernatural peace that guards your heart from being overwhelmed with worry! He promises to do so. And oh yes …, one other thing you might consider while your praying for them and giving them over once again to the mighty hand of God. Listen to Russell one more time say … "Don't worry, they'll be back … more troubles than they left with." The key is to not worry, if troubles come back with them count them as blessings and watch what the Lord will do.

M & M'S – NOT CANDY
BUT A MIRROR

2000-2007

I BELIEVE THAT THE MEN AND women that serving in the areas of public safety are remarkable. I am speaking of those in our military, fire and para-medic services, physicians and, of cores, law enforcement. It is this last category that will occupy some of our story here.

As I have mentioned in previous chapters the work God has done in raising up the ministry of Calvary Chapel Valley Springs remains a glorious mystery to me. There are many people who God worked in and through that have come and gone but are still in my view. I'd like to share about two men, both with law enforcement backgrounds, both carry the first name of Mike. Hence the title for this chapter M & M's. I'll explain the mirror portion of the title as we go.

I recall it was late in the year 1999. My wife, Sherry, and I had stretched ourselves to the limit with work, family and starting a ministry. Sherry continued to educate children in the local Elementary School, spending time counseling women and serving in Children's Ministries each Sunday. I would work as a union meet cutter to help make ends meet. Spending the balance of my time counseling men, reaching out to new families in the community and preparing for each Bible study and Sunday messages.

In the middle of those things, we both also tried to keep a small "youth group" a float by meeting with Jr High School and High School age kids one night a week. It was exciting, fun, challenging and exhausting all at the same time. After about a year of it we both hit the preverbal wall and began to wonder what to do next. You might even say we were desperate to see what God would do next because we knew something needed to change. I remember hearing God's "...still small voice" (1 Kings 19:12) saying: "...your done with this part of your ministry, it's time to pass it on!"

During a conversation with a dear colleague and friend, Bill Beckleman, senior pastor at Calvary Chapel Coastlands, whom I'd prayed with weekly I mentioned our dilemma and asked for more prayer. It wasn't long before Bill mentioned a man, he'd met that he knew was praying about serving God in ministry. There weren't any lightening bolts from heaven or a parting of the skies when the suggestion was made to call him. Just a still, small voice that nudged me to follow through and investigate who this man might be. We exchanged the phone number and as soon as I hung up from Bill, I shot up a quick, genuine cry for the Lord's direction and dialed the number.

Answering the other end of the line was a man answered with a kind hello. I introduced myself, explained how I had gotten his contact information and asked if he had a few minutes for me. The answer was " ...sure go a head!" What takes place next is clearly miraculous.

Mike Scanlan, the first of our M's in this story, listened as I shared my personal testimony and God's call to the Valley Springs area. I explained that we had been given specific direction from Scripture about this place and that we had planted the church. It came from Psalm 84:5-6 which says, *"Blessed is the man whose strength is in You, whose heart is set on pilgrimage. As they pass through the **Valley** of Baca, They make it a **spring**; The rain also covers it with pools."* Years earlier God had spoken these words to us and taught us to trust Him that this was where He wanted us to serve. I then turned my attention to Mike. I asked him to share about himself.

As I listened, I heard a man passionately desiring to serve God. At that time, Mike was a sergeant for the Long Beach PD and had been with the department for many years. He'd come to faith and was actively sharing his faith with others in the department. He'd begun serving at Calvary Chapel Costa Mesa in various ways and attending multiple bible studies in a desire to grow in biblical knowledge and God's grace. Then it happened! A strong prompting came over me and I asked this man I barely knew a question. I asked him if he would pray about leaving his career, his home and familiar surroundings and come to Valley Springs to serve in Youth Ministries. I couldn't offer him an income and I couldn't guarantee him a place to live but there were young people awaiting attention and care if he was willing. As we ended our call he agreed to pray about the matter, and we said goodbye. I somewhat expected to not hear from him for quite a while.

How long do you think it was before I heard back from Mike? In a word: hours. Yep, as I recall it was only a few hours later. The phone rang. Mike explained that he and his wife, Grace, had gone to separate rooms in the house to seek the Lord. As they prayed separately for direction God spoke one united word. Go! Through multiple verses in scripture God had confirmed that this was the time to step out in faith and go! They were willing and were ready to leave all for the adventure of a lifetime.

Miraculous in some way? Absolutely! Consistent with who our God is when He finds willing vessels? No doubt! The Scanlan's proceeded to place their home on the market, which sold in three days. Mike gave his notice at the department and, in a little over month, they were on Interstate 5, headed north in a U-Hall soon to arrive at our home.

The night that they arrived was wet, cold and windy. Some of us from the church met at a garage that would serve as a temporary storage unit until they found permanent lodging. Then we drove the U-Hal with his bed over to our home. I remember saying to Mike, " … we can put you guys up for a bit but where are you going to live?" His answer was as classic as it gets! He calmly replied; "I don't know but the Lord will provide!" They were living out the promise that Jesus gives each one of His followers in the gospels about trust! Do you know it?

Jesus said: "Therefore I say to you, do not worry about your life, what you will eat or what you will drink; nor about your body, what you will put on. Is not life more than food and the body more than clothing? Which of you by worrying can add one cubit to his stature? Therefore do not worry, saying, 'What shall we eat?'

or 'What shall we drink?' or 'What shall we wear?' ...
For your heavenly Father knows that you need all these
things. But seek first the kingdom of God and His
righteousness, and all these things shall be added to
you. (Matt 6:25,27,3, 32b,33)

Are you worrying about your tomorrow's today? Are you
overly concerned about what you will eat, the clothing
you will wear or how you will be cared for in the future?
Is the Lord asking you to step out in faith in a given area
of service to Him? We can all live and learn from the
Scanlan's testimony.

The beautiful and ironic thing about Mike's trust in the
Lord to fulfill His promise is that He fulfilled it through
my wife and I. For the next three years our home was
a shared home with our new co-laborers in Christ. We
eventually ordained Mike into the ministry and his
call to leave Law Enforcement and serve as a pastor
was realized here at Calvary Chapel Valley Springs.
After seven years of serving together in ministry the
Scanlan's moved on to take on a small Calvary Chapel
in the Susanville area where Mike still serves as the
senior pastor.

Oh yes, you might ask about the meaning of the *mirror*
in the title of this chapter? I will simply say that Mike's
life and commitment to serving Christ was, and remains,

always a constant "mirror" to me. When I observe my brother and his passion for God, I can often see the places the Lord wants to strengthen in my own relationship with Himself and calling me to a deeper trust in His word and promises.

We are reminded in the book of James to: "*...be doers of the word, and not hearers only, deceiving yourselves. For if anyone is a hearer of the word and not a doer, he is like a man observing his natural face in a **mirror**; ... for he observes himself, goes away, and immediately forgets what kind of man he was. But he who looks into the perfect law of liberty and continues in it, and is not a forgetful hearer but a doer of the work, this one will be blessed in what he does.*" (James 1:22-25)

Who is a "mirror" of God's faithfulness in your life today? Are you observing and then forgetting or remembering all God has said? Perhaps it is time to look again with a new set of eyes?

MIKE VENEMAN
(MV) – ANOTHER M
-ANOTHER MIRROR

2004 -2007

THE SECOND OF OUR M's is a man named Mike Veneman, we'll refer to him as MV. Also with a law enforcement background, MV was actively employed with the Police Department in Stockton, California when I met him. The church in Valley Springs had been up and running for a few years and starting to grow.

It is always amazing to watch God whisper into the ear of men and women that already have a relationship with Jesus Christ. Often that whisper will come in the form of an invitation to get to know Him better. How well would you say that you know Jesus? Does He call you friend? The bible declares it so! As a friend of God, can you say that you know Him well? These are the kind of questions that were running through the heart and mind of Mike Veneman when our lives intersected. Let me explain.

Back then, by Mike's own word, on Sunday's he was satisfied with a little bit of Jesus, and then on to a little bit of Football. Going to church once a week was, in his mind, enough as a Christian. Oh, I'm sure there was "some" bible reading from week to week but his job as an investigator, his responsibilities as a husband and father occupied most of his time. Sunday was a "day-off." This was when he got to do what "he wanted" to do in his free time! Once his "go-in to church" duties were fulfilled it was on to other things.

For various reasons the Veneman family decided to visit Calvary Chapel Valley Springs (CCVS). The previous church had served a purpose in their lives but God was prompting them forward to something new. It would prove to be a dramatically new thing that God did in their entire household. MV tells the story very well.

Mike relates that upon their entrance into a makeshift sanctuary in a multi-purpose room at an Elementary School something began to happen during the worship services. The songs being sung seem to penetrate their hearts in a new way. The passion with which others were engaged in the worship of God moved them greatly. During their first visits and subsequent worship services they saw themselves in need of personal revival and were immediately drawn closer to the Lord. It was beginning to look like CCVS would be the Veneman's new church home.

One of my privileges as a pastor is to encourage God's people to love and good works. When I meet a new family that is visiting from another church I welcome them, pray with them, and ask God to lead them in their search. Over the next few weeks, I got to know Mike and his wife, Tracy, better. Conversations almost always ended in a discussion of spiritual things and God's desire for our lives. I could tell they were hungry for the deep things of God. They loved to worship the Lord and were gifted in areas of music and singing. We observed their lives for about 6 months and then the obvious came to fruition. Both joined the worship team. Their teen age children got deeply involved in our youth group and our youth pastors' life. (See previous M) And the momentum of change for the Veneman family began.

As a worship team, including myself, during times of rehearsal we would spend many evenings simply at the feet of Jesus. One night, as I recall it, I gave Mike and Tracy a gentle challenge. I said; "you both seem to have often sung "ABOUT" the Lord but have you ever really sung "TO" Him?" As Mike tells it that was "it" for them. I'll quote him here: "From that time forward

we never would want for this world as we did before."
It was in those rehearsals that we would get lost in
His presence and cry out together for the overflow of
His Spirit to fill us all afresh. Prayer for the church, its
direction and its people were always at the core of our
time together. The music was only the window through
which our access to His graces were encountered. They
were wonderful times.

Over the years that followed, the Veneman family
became fully engulfed in God's work there in the Valley
Springs area and CCVS. And then it happened again.
Mike's desires were changing. No longer was Sunday a
"day-off!" Football did not have the same appeal it once
had. Sunday was the Lord's Day and a day of ministry.
No longer was it a little bit of Jesus but Mike wanted
"ALL" that Jesus had for him. He began to wonder about
the call on his life to full time ministry.

A School of Ministry (SoM) opportunity opened in a city
nearby. After seeking the Lord with his wife and family
Mike applied. He was accepted as a student, made the
necessary adjustments at work to attend and continued
in law enforcement. The SoM classes lasted two years.
During that time Mike believed he was being called
to pastoral ministry. At the end of classes Mike was
ordination and the Veneman's were sent out to take on a
Calvary Chapel in Livermore, CA where Mike served as

its pastor for ten years. God's call upon Mike's life to full time ministry was ignited here at CCVS and brought to fruition during his time at SoM. We are forever thankful to the Lord for His faithfulness. And ever grateful to have a part in the calling and sending of His servants into the world. Change again has brought Mike and his family to an assisting pastoral role at Calvary Chapel of Modesto under the leadership of pastor Damian Kyle. And now you might ask, but what about the mirror?

MV's experience and testimony is again a constant mirror to me. It is a simple picture of what God can do when we worship Him in Spirit and in Truth. It reflects the fact that God can speak to us as we worship Him! It is a reminder that we can all find ourselves in need of revival. At which point the singing of a simple song, filled with a passionate heart, cried out in the privacy of a living room, out in nature or the sanctuary of a church can be the spark the ignites the flame of God's Spirit within!

Are you satisfied with a little bit of Jesus and a little bit of other things? Are you always working for that day-off? Is your worship of God filled with passion? Are you singing about Him or are you singing to Him? Are you in need of revival? Let's remember what our Lord promised; "Ask, and it will be given to you; seek, and you will find; knock, and it will be opened to you." (Mt 7:7)

DUDLEY MEYER – INSIGHTS TO INTERSESSION

1999-2013

"...The effective, fervent prayer of a righteous man avails much. Elijah was a man with a nature like ours, and he prayed earnestly that it would not rain; and it did not rain on the land for three years and six months. And he prayed again, and the heaven gave rain, and the earth produced its fruit. (James 5:16b-18)

It was Christmas Eve around 1966. My brother and his girlfriend invited me to join them at a Catholic Church Mass. I knew nothing about the Bible or salvation at this time. I understood nothing about the concept of God except, that there probably was One somewhere out there! After all, I was only in 7th Grade and had had no religious upbringing.

When we entered the church, it was a solemn experience for me. The stained-glass cathedral with its ornate pews and pulpit, the crucifix hanging center stage all gave this young boy the sense that perhaps God was here if he was anywhere!

As the Catholic priest began the mass there were segments of something called: "prayer". It was difficult for me to understand what I was to do. If you've ever been a non-Catholic, un-churched individual at your first Catholic Mass you'll get what I mean. Was I supposed to join in the praying or just listen as someone else prays? Some of those prayers may have even been in a foreign language. I would find out later it was Latin. The subject of prayer seemed odd, un-understandable and strange.

It would be many years later that a profoundly true and deep understanding of prayer would be made known to me. Unknown to me as a young boy, prayer does have a genuine impact upon human lives and the heart of God. These things were made even clearer to me one day over a lunch shared and the testimony of a dear brother named Dudley. Allow me to share it with you.

Dudley Meyer and his wife, Erna, had come to live in San Andreas, near Valley Springs, California in the winter of 1999 because he was hired by the Calaveras

County Assessor's office. They were interested in Calvary Chapel Valley Springs and wanted to get to know me a bit more personally, so Dudley and I scheduled a lunch together.

I came to find out that the Meyer's had moved there from the beautiful high Sierra Town of Truckee. Truckee is the "out-of-doors" man's ultimate playground. Complete with its beautiful trails and camping sites in the summer to its near by high ski slopes in the winter. One can find endless ways to enjoy the beauty of God's mountains there. As a Jeep enthusiast, Dudley had taken advantage of the many places to drive "off-road." It was in Truckee that he spent twenty-one years as a loving husband, raising his two daughters, providing for his household and, uniquely, it was there he also came to a living faith in Christ. By using the term "living faith" I would simply remind the reader that there may be many who believe in God and agree that Jesus is the Son of God, died for the sin of mankind and rose the third day. But when those truths are being lived out in a passion and love for the Savior, we would refer to that as a living faith! Through the faithful ministry of pastor Brian Larson of Calvary Chapel of Truckee, the Meyer family grew in their love for God and His word. Then something happened that catapulted Dudley deep into a life of prayer. I'll explain.

As I recall it was 1988. CC Truckee was to take part in a short-term mission trip to China to deliver bibles and other helps to the underground church. There would be some dangers involved. Being caught with illegal contraband in China never goes well for anyone foreign or domestic. Dudley had a desire to go but it was through Erna's submission to God and her willingness to encourage her husband that this adventure of faith would materialize. He would join the team and go.

Having been on trips myself I felt the intensity of his hopes and expectations while he shared the experience with me. I was often the one in the rented vehicle, pioneering a team through streets and even jungle to arrive at a pre-arranged location. I had known the thrill of delivering bibles to the underground church in Viet Nam. Needed foods in Mexico and help repair facilities in the Philippines.

Dudley was hopeful and envisioned himself, along with the others in the team, delivering bibles, sharing the Gospel. They could not meet with underground church leaders due to the high risk of their persecution! But it would all be glorying in the work of God during the accomplishment of this mission! I get it! As I listened to hear of the adventure's details I was on the edge of my seat! Where did he go? Who did he meet? What cities were they in? I was amazed at his answer.

After the long flight overseas to China, the team arrived at their "base" accommodations in Shenzhen, 15 miles north of Hong Kong. It was a small multi-family apartment that would serve its purpose. Each one checked into their rooms and Phase one was complete.

At a meeting the next morning, the Truckee team was introduced to the Australian coordinator of Brother Andrew's Open Doors ministry. He and his associates would explain the process of entry into China and delivering bibles to pre-arranged destinations. One of his associates was an 80-year-old gentleman. For more than 20-years this man was a pastor in the U.S. and following that he was 20-years the headmaster of a Bible school he founded in Mindanao, Philippines.

The moment came for departure when Dudley was delivered a life changing directive. An element of secrecy was necessary to keep the Bible couriers and Underground Church leaders safe. The old man announced to the group, saying Dudley and I will remain here in Shenzhen praying while the remainder of the team, with Bibles, crosses the border into China. In other words, Dudley's contribution to phase two was to provide the "prayer covering" for the rest of the team.

There in a foreign country, with high hopes of further travel and adventures for the glory of God, this young man finds himself relegated to staying alone in the apartment with an old man to pray. In his thoughts, Dudley was secretly asking the Lord to teach him to pray because he didn't know how, seriously.

As Dudley explained to me what happened I was almost devastated for him. But, as he continued, the glimmer in his eyes convinced me that this momentarily dashed expectation was actually a tremendous life altering opportunity! In his own words Dudley tells of the adventure:

"Ten couriers loaded up with Bibles and departed, leaving us behind. Then the old man said something like, "okay, let's get to work and pray." Together we sat, quietly, in repose at the dining room table; minutes went by without a spoken word; more wordless minutes went by.

In a slightly audible tone, the old man spoke and said, Almighty God – El Shaddai. With those few words God's Holy Spirit filled the room with His unmistakable presence. There is no remembrance of what we prayed during the next 6 hours."

There in that room the God of all Creation, in the Person of the Holy Spirit met him and taught him a new and living way of engaging in dialogue with our Savior. It became a " ...holy unto the Lord" time for them both.

I was reminded of the apostle Paul's promise to the Christians in Rome.

"Likewise the Spirit also helps in our weaknesses. For we do not know what we should pray for as we ought, but the Spirit Himself makes intercession for us with groanings which cannot be uttered. Now He who searches the hearts knows what the mind of the Spirit is, because He makes intercession for the saints according to the will of God." (Romans 8:26-27).

By a work of the Spirit of God, Dudley's life, his heavenly perspectives and his ministry would forever be changed. He had entered the ministry of Intersession.

Dudley finished his story by telling me that the entire team returned home, phase three, and yes, it was all for the glory of God. All of them believing that the prayers of the saints secured its success. I was then, and remain today, in awe at what God had done and how He did it in the life of one of His servants.

I will take a bit of liberty here and draw two parallels from Scriptures. There are examples in our Bible of men and women who possessed a relationship with God but would soon be called deeper into that same relationship. One such example is Moses. Called by God at one point to be a deliverer for the people of Israel but sent to fulfill that call some forty years later.

The turning point for him was an encounter with the living God at the burning bush. For it was there that God spoke to Moses and Moses spoke with God for the first time. We can read the exchange: Then Moses said to God, "Indeed, when I come to the children of Israel and say to them, 'The God of your fathers has sent me to you,' and they say to me, 'What is His name?' what shall I say to them?" And God said to Moses, "I AM WHO I AM." And He said, "Thus you shall say to the children of Israel, 'I AM has sent me to you.'"(Exodus 3:13-14).

Moses' call and his commission were given and received! Moses was changed forever! He too learned to be an intercessor for God's people.

I can also mention the Spirit of God speaking to Peter on the roof top at Joppa. Peter possessed a relationship with the Lord, but God wanted to deepen that relationship. How would God do it? It would begin in a time of prayer.

While he was in prayer on the roof top, he fell into a state of half sleep and half awake. God showed him things and spoke to him. In that dream state Peter was at first confused about what was going on but it wasn't long that Peter came to realize that the Spirit was teaching him things he needed to learn. How so? In times of prayer. The Lord wanted to deepen Peter's understanding that God has created all men, and none should be called unclean so that the Gospel could go further through is life. To which Peter was led to the house of Cornelius, a Gentile, and Peter's life, ministry and heavenly perspectives changed forever as well. (Read Acts 10)

An apartment in a foreign country had become a burning bush, a roof-top moment, a place where a man who walked with God would now walk more closely. It had become a sanctuary where intercession for the saints would rise to God's throne as a sweet-smelling aroma.

As Dudley finished sharing his testimony of the trip and its impact on his life, I was forever changed as well. I came to a greater realization of the need for intercession in my own life. I also was overjoyed that God had brought such dear brother, and his family into our midst. My wife and I, my entire family and my ministry remain the beneficiaries of their intersession. Thank you, Lord.

Did you know there is some One praying for you right now? Oh yes. And that One knows exactly how to pray for you. Take comfort in this: *"Who shall bring a charge against God's elect? It is God who justifies. Who is he who condemns? It is Christ who died, and furthermore is also risen, who is even at the right hand of God, who also makes intercession for us.* (Rom.8:33-34) Yes, it is Jesus Christ interceding for you right now!

I close with some questions. What is prayer to you? Have you found it to be something you're not sure of how to do? Ask God to teach you. He will. Have you viewed prayer as the lesser of activities in reaching the world or your neighborhood for Christ? Perhaps, like many of us, we see the ability to send a check or packaged items, take a short-term trip to bring food and bibles as our contribution to the Great Commission. But intercessory prayer is of it self a great work to further the kingdoms of God.

Is God calling you deeper into that relationship you already possess? We don't need to travel to a bland hotel room in a foreign country and be relegated to its four walls to know the joys of intimate and deeper dialogue with God. We don't need to be on a "missions' trip" to become intercessor's Start right where you are. Start today. Start tonight.

POST SCRIPT

I would like to close with a question and some comments. How is your living going? How is your learning going? Are the important lessons you learn finding their way into a more productive and fruitful life? The greater question is this: Does God have your ear and your attention? Does He have your heart? If He were to try and teach you something that would change your life, your direction or your ultimate passion would He find you willing to learn from Him?

At times the lessons learned in this life can be very difficult or even painful. Not all lessons are difficult or painful, but every lesson given to us by God is intended to increase our hope for today and for tomorrow. As Paul reminded the Christians in Rome: " ...For whatever things were written before were written for our learning, that we through the patience and comfort of the Scriptures might have hope." (Ro 15:4)

It would indeed be an unfortunate thing to, as 2 Timothy 3:7 tells us, " ...always learning and never able to come to the knowledge of the truth."

Thus, my exhortation throughout this book is with the loving intent that you and I may always be open to the things that God would want to teach us. And that by those things we would live and learn to learn and live.

Printed in the United States
by Baker & Taylor Publisher Services